WHY MUST WE
FORGIVE?

✖ CULTIVATING BIBLICAL GODLINESS

Series Editors
Joel R. Beeke and Ryan M. McGraw

Dr. D. Martyn Lloyd-Jones once said that what the church needs to do most of all is "to begin herself to live the Christian life. If she did that, men and women would be crowding into our buildings. They would say, 'What is the secret of this?'" As Christians, one of our greatest needs is for the Spirit of God to cultivate biblical godliness in us in order to put the beauty of Christ on display through us, all to the glory of the triune God. With this goal in mind, this series of booklets treats matters vital to Christian experience at a basic level. Each booklet addresses a specific question in order to inform the mind, warm the affections, and transform the whole person by the Spirit's grace, so that the church may adorn the doctrine of God our Savior in all things.

WHY MUST WE
FORGIVE?

**Forgiveness Received
and Reciprocated**

STANLEY D. GALE

REFORMATION HERITAGE BOOKS
GRAND RAPIDS, MICHIGAN

Why Must We Forgive?
© 2015 by Stanley D. Gale

Reformation Heritage Books
2965 Leonard St. NE
Grand Rapids, MI 49525
616-977-0889 / Fax 616-285-3246
orders@heritagebooks.org
www.heritagebooks.org

Printed in the United States of America
15 16 17 18 19 20/10 9 8 7 6 5 4 3 2 1

ISBN 978-1-60178-417-9

WHY MUST WE
FORGIVE?
———✕———

This was her second meeting with the counselor. Ellen attended Sunday worship and was active in her church, but something was stifling her spiritual growth and contentment. It had gotten worse in recent months, so she had sought help from a Christian counselor.

A couple of sessions in, it came out that Ellen had been abused as a child. Clearly, she was wracked with pain over the experience. The counselor tried to get her to open up and to express the hurt, still fresh after all these years.

But Ellen would have nothing of it. When the counselor probed, she didn't merely skirt the subject; she guarded it like a pit bull. She made it clear that she hated her father and would never forgive him. In fact, she would not even consider the prospect.

As she met with the counselor over the next few months, Ellen was willing to talk about everything but the abuse. It was like the counselor had free rein of the house—except for one room at the center. On the door to that room was a circle. Within the circle stood a cross, a diagonal line drawn across it. No one admitted. Not even Jesus.

There is something wrong with that picture, something that reaches to the heart of the Christian faith, something that undermines, or at least underestimates, the power of the gospel itself. Jesus taught His disciples to pray, "Forgive us our debts, as we forgive our debtors" (Matt. 6:12). Paul urged the followers of Christ to forgive one another. Even as Christ forgave them, they were to forgive (Col. 3:13). Christ gives us our mandate and our model for the forgiveness necessary for healing and health in relationships, as expressive of the gospel. But what is forgiveness, and how is it practiced? We can grasp God's direction for us under two headings: forgiveness received and forgiveness reciprocated.

FORGIVENESS RECEIVED
Foundation of Forgiveness
A recent article reported that 35 percent of Americans have debt in collections. It is no surprise to hear of Americans in debt. What is startling is to hear that over a third of the population is in debt to such a degree that their accounts have been closed and turned over to collection agencies to recoup what they can. But for those in the kingdom of God, there is no such debt. Every citizen of heaven is debt-free. We're not talking about financial liability. We are referring to the debt of sin.

Our sins put us in a position of accountability to God. That debt accrues every time we transgress God's law, whether in thought, in word, or in deed, in things done or left undone. Have we been angry with our brother in our heart? We have sinned. Have we loved self or possessions more than we have loved God? We have added to our debt.

But the glory of the gospel is that though the wages of sin is death, the gift of God is eternal life in Christ Jesus our Lord (Rom. 6:23). As citizens of heaven, our debt has not been canceled like the debt a Third World country might owe to its creditor, a more prosperous nation. Nor has it been pardoned like a convicted criminal having his death sentence commuted by the governor—in which case the guilt of sin remains, but its consequence is removed.

No, the gospel is the good news not that the debt of sin owed has been canceled or pardoned, but that it has been paid—in full. When it comes to the debt of sin before a holy God who must punish iniquity, we cannot pay it down through some sort of payment arrangement. We cannot negotiate a lesser obligation. We cannot escape through bankruptcy. Our debt must be paid because God's divine justice must be satisfied. He would be less than holy, less than God, were He not to exact full payment.

That is what the cross of Christ is all about. Jesus was born under law to redeem those under law. He came to pay the debt of our sin. He gave His life as a ransom for many. On the cross He uttered words of legal transaction: "It is finished." The sense is that the debt is paid. The books are cleared for those He came to redeem, not by any trick of accounting but by payment in full for all sins past, present, and future.

The anthem of the believer is this:

My sin—oh, the bliss of this glorious thought!—
My sin, not in part, but the whole,
Is nailed to the cross, and I bear it no more;
Praise the Lord, praise the Lord, O my soul![1]

By grace, through faith in Christ, believers are debt-free, always and forever. God has provided no other means for the remission of sins, no other avenue for debt forgiveness.

Drinking from the Fountain of Forgiveness

The good news of the gospel proclaims that those who have taken refuge in Christ stand forgiven of the entirety of their debt of sin. Jesus paid it all. All to Him we owe. That does not mean, however, that the blood of Christ bankrolls our sin. Any such notion prompts the apostle Paul to say, aghast, "Shall we continue in sin, that grace may abound? God forbid" (Rom. 6:1–2). The very thought is abhorrent and an abomination to grace.

What part, then, does forgiveness play in our ongoing relationship with God? How does the positional forgiveness of justification relate to the progressive forgiveness of sanctification as we die to sin and live to righteousness? To put it in practical

---

1. Horatio G. Spafford, "It Is Well with My Soul," stanza 3.

terms: Why must we ask God for forgiveness if we already stand completely and continually forgiven by Him?

In his first epistle, the apostle John helps us find our answers. Writing to believers, he emphatically states: "If we say that we have no sin, we deceive ourselves, and the truth is not in us" (1 John 1:8). Lest we think we misread, he says it again, this time making it personal with God: "If we say that we have not sinned, we make him a liar, and his word is not in us" (1 John 1:10).

What is John talking about? He is saying that we as Christians continue to sin. If we think otherwise, we deceive ourselves. A realistic view of self in the mirror of God's Word will see the sulliedness of sin. John says nothing more surprising than what Paul says in Romans 7, where he relates his personal struggle with sin even after providing detailed reasoning that Christ had freed him from sin's guilt and power (Romans 3–6). Believers sin. To refuse to acknowledge that of ourselves is to call God a liar and expose that perhaps we are not Christians at all. The truth is not in us, John says.

Once acknowledged, sin must be confessed. Sandwiched in between the bread of God's truth in 1 John 1:8 and 10—that we continue to sin—is the meat of John's point that we must confess that sin. "If we confess our sins, he is faithful and just to forgive us our sins, and to cleanse us from all unrighteousness" (1 John 1:9). These words both assure and puzzle us, stirring in us both comfort and confusion. It is wonderful to know that forgiveness is ours for the asking. But why do we need to confess at all, and what do God's faithfulness and justice have to do with it?

To "confess" is to align ourselves with God. Literally, the word John uses, *homologeo*, means to say (*logeo*) the same thing (*homo*). To confess sin means we call our actions or inactions what God calls them: not mere mistakes, not indiscretions, but sin—intentional or unintentional violations of the law of God. The psalmist puts confession in terms of acknowledging our transgressions:

> Blessed is he whose transgression is forgiven, whose sin is covered. Blessed is the man unto whom the LORD imputeth not iniquity, and in whose spirit there is no guile.... I acknowledged my sin unto thee, and mine iniquity have I not hid. I said, I will confess my transgressions unto the LORD; and thou forgavest the iniquity of my sin. (Ps. 32:1–2, 5)

We uncover our sin, admitting it, refusing to hide it by rationalizations, blame shifting, or euphemism. In turn, God covers it by no longer imputing iniquity, not reckoning debt.

This transaction of grace is founded on the basis of God's granting forgiveness when we confess our sin. John tells us that God is "faithful and just to forgive us our sins." We can understand "faithful." God is true to His character and to His word. But why "just"? We would have expected John to say faithful and *merciful* to forgive, not just.

But "just" captures the transaction involved in forgiveness. The debt is paid. God's justice has been satisfied. Where and how was that done? At the cross. In the first two verses of chapter 2, John continues his thought: "My little children, these things write I unto you, that ye sin not. And if any man sin, we have an advocate with the Father, Jesus Christ the righteous: and he is the propitiation for our sins: and not for ours only, but also for the sins of the whole world" (1 John 2:1–2).

What that tells us is that *forgiveness is not found in mere confession of sin, but in confession of Christ*. Jesus is our advocate, our defense attorney, against the accusations of Satan. Our spiritual adversary points out our sin. Jesus counters that though the sin is real, He atoned for it. Our enemy the devil draws our attention to the abundance or heinousness of sin in our lives to drive us to despair. The Holy Spirit, however, convicts us of that sin to draw us to Christ. This distinction helps us to stand firm in Christ for the spiritual battle we face as part of the Christian life against the enemy of our souls (see Zech. 3:1–5; Eph. 6:10–12; Rev. 12:10).

Jesus is the righteous One, the One who gave Himself, the Just for the unjust. He is the propitiation for our sins, the One who paid the penalty for them, the One who endured the wrath of God they deserved. In confession, we draw on the inexhaustible riches of God's grace, bound up in our justification.

We can't tell an unbeliever to confess sin with the assurance he or she will be forgiven by virtue of that confession. Forgiveness is bound up in Christ alone. That's why John says that Jesus is "the propitiation for our sins: and not for ours only, but also for the sins of the whole world" (1 John 2:2). God has provided no other way to pay the debt of sin and to escape its consequences than the giving of His Son. He is the only way of reconciliation for Jew and Gentile alike—the whole world.

How is sin different for believers and unbelievers? In one sense, sin is sin. It is rebellion against God, transgression of His law, disobedience to His revealed will. The difference is that for believers sin is atoned for. Their guilt is removed. The debt is paid. Unbelievers, however, remain saddled with the guilt of their sin and continue to accrue debt that must be settled at the judgment seat of God.

Our sin *as believers* affects our fellowship with God, but not our relationship. When my children disobey me, I don't stop being their father. In fact, it is as their father that I deal with their sin in love. When we sin, we turn our backs on God to follow after sin. But God still loves us. John remarks on this love: "Behold, what manner of love the Father hath bestowed upon us, that we should be called the sons of God" (1 John 3:1). We can know ourselves as "beloved," called to love Him who first loved us.

That means we as believers confess our sins, not as sinners to the Judge, but as children to our Father. Confession does not return us to God's good grace but turns us back to God's face, from which we turned away to follow after sin. We cannot invite unbelievers to confess their sin without confessing the Christ who is the end of sin.

But there's more that our God wants of us. He wants us to forgive *as we have been forgiven by Him.* As believers who have received forgiveness, He calls us to reciprocate.

FORGIVENESS RECIPROCATED
The Flow of Forgiveness

Jesus relates a disturbing story in which a servant is forgiven an enormous debt but in turn refuses to reciprocate by forgiving a much lesser debt owed him. Our Lord told this parable to show God's design for forgiveness. Jesus had laid out steps for those sinned against to pursue reconciliation (Matt. 18:15–20). Evidently, that teaching prompted a question from Peter: "Lord, how oft shall my brother sin against me, and I forgive him? till seven times?" (Matt. 18:21). Peter likely thought he was being magnanimous by expressing willingness to forgive seven times. Jesus, however, used the accounting principle of grace: "I say not unto thee, Until seven times: but, Until seventy times seven" (Matt. 18:22).

That's when Jesus launched into His parable of kingdom economics. He describes a king who was owed a ridiculous sum by one of his servants. It would be like a middle-class American owing many millions of dollars. The king takes pity on the servant and liberates him from the debt. That same servant, however, encounters one who owes him money, a substantial amount but not exorbitant, something in the order of three years' wages. The second servant pleads for pity, but the first servant will have nothing of it. He orders the one in his debt to be ripped from family and home and remanded to the custody of the jailer until the debt is paid.

By this parable, Jesus is not commending the Golden Rule, "Do unto others as you would have them do unto you." He is describing how forgiveness is to function in the kingdom of God. We are to "pay it forward," dealing in the currency that we have received. He is answering Peter's question in terms different from Peter's asking, making the king's remarkable forgiveness the standard and point of reference. That's why the spreadsheet of forgiveness is so extraordinary. It is not governed by customary banking practices but by the unreasonable expanse of grace.

But what shocks us is Jesus' bottom line: "So likewise shall my heavenly Father do also unto you, if ye from your hearts forgive not every one his brother their trespasses" (Matt. 18:35). Is Jesus telling us that the forgiveness we received can be rescinded? Can the debt of our sin be reinstated? To put it bluntly, can we lose our salvation?

The introductory word "so" in Jesus' bottom line speaks not to logical consequence (e.g., therefore) but to example (e.g., in this manner). He is not issuing a threat but making a point. It is akin to His instruction in the prayer He teaches His disciples: "Forgive us our debts, as we forgive our debtors" (Matt. 6:12). He is laying out for us the reciprocity of forgiveness in kingdom exchange. We who have been forgiven much should always be prepared to forgive little. Any offense will be *little* compared to that forgiven us by our God. We might think it much, but that will only be because we have lost our bearings in the gospel of the kingdom accounting practices.

Is there legitimacy in taking Jesus' statement as a reference to one's salvation? Philip Ryken, in his commentary on the Lord's Prayer, believes so. He says, "The ability to forgive is one of the surest signs of having been forgiven. It is proof that we have received God's grace. Those who are truly forgiven, truly forgive."[2] For Ryken, persistent unwillingness to forgive does not suggest that we can lose our salvation, but that we never possessed it. Charles Spurgeon says the same thing in stark terms: "Unless you have forgiven others, you read your own death warrant when you repeat the Lord's Prayer."[3]

---

2. Philip Graham Ryken, *When You Pray* (Phillipsburg, N.J.: P&R, 2000), 138.

3. As quoted in Ryken, *When You Pray*, 137.

These are sobering words that Ellen needs to hear in her refusal to forgive her abusive father. The point is not merely the act of forgiveness, but her openness to take it up in obedience to the Lord who gave His life to purchase her forgiveness. She needs to remove the sign from the door of her heart she refused to open to Christ. There can be no areas of our lives to which the lordship of Jesus is off limits.

This is not to minimize the horrors of abuse or the indelible trauma it can cause. It is to say that even as horrific as abuse is, its guilt and power are not beyond the scope of the gospel or the healing properties of God's grace.

A word of caution is in order. We don't want to be rash or presumptuous in declaring those who refuse to forgive to be unbelievers, but it is cause for circumspection. When we see in our own hearts hesitancy—if not unwillingness—to forgive those who sin against us, we see the need for a refresher course in the gospel. We want to take stock of the debt of our sin forgiven by God through the giving of His Son. It calls us to a different vantage point, seeing the log in our own eye before addressing the speck in another's.

Our Lord Jesus speaks of forgiveness "from your hearts" (Matt. 18:35). A heart *awash* with awe of God's forgiveness, *accosted* by the unreasonable grace of God in its doing, and *aware* of its cost in the giving of His Son will be inclined to operate on the principles of kingdom economics.

Exactly how do we apply these principles? What is forgiveness, and how do we practice it in our dealing with those who have sinned against us, those in our debt?

Forgiveness in Action

We want to grasp first what forgiveness is before we can explore how to go about its practice. Two Greek words help us in understanding forgiveness.

The first word (in order of address, not importance) is *aphiemi*. This is the term used by our Lord in Matthew 6:12 when He teaches us to ask our Father in heaven to forgive our debts as we forgive our debtors. It is also the word Peter uses when he asks Jesus how many times it is appropriate to forgive.

The thrust of this term is to let go, dismiss, or drop. When someone sins against us, it is like we are given a promissory note of debt, payable on demand. To dismiss it is to tear it up. If someone lashes out at me in anger, spewing insults and hurtful speech, that person is in my debt. I have a hold over him. He has wronged me. When I forgive, I let loose that hold. I drop the ammunition I had against him. It is no longer available to me as a weapon. We cannot just holster the weapon; we must discard it.

The other word translated *forgive* in the Greek New Testament is *charizomai*. We find this term at the core of Paul's charter of Christian unity:

> Put on therefore, as the elect of God, holy and beloved, bowels of mercies, kindness, humbleness

of mind, meekness, longsuffering; forbearing one another, and forgiving one another, if any man have a quarrel against any: even as Christ forgave you, so also do ye. And above all these things put on charity, which is the bond of perfectness. (Col. 3:12–14)

This word puts a positive spin on forgiveness. Its root is *charis*, grace. In forgiving, we give grace. We let the offense go not because the offender deserves it, but as an act of grace. We forgive as we have been forgiven. We forgive in the model Jesus calls for in His parable, looking first to the grace we have received. Our action is driven not by just desert, but by the exercise of gracious generosity. We cancel the debt as an act of willful love (charity).

These two terms frame the starting point, the posture for the exercise of forgiveness. Whenever someone approaches us to ask for our forgiveness, we want to harken to the debt of our own sin so graciously forgiven us. The only way we can get our bearings for undertaking *aphiemi* and *charizomai* is to reflect on God's grace to us in canceling the debt of our sin and the ransom He paid to do so. Without those bearings, we will be puffed up in pride and think ourselves other than the sinners saved by grace that we are.

Now, having grasped what forgiveness is, how do we go about dispensing it? We can boil it down to two actions.

First, to forgive is to no longer hold the offense against the person who sinned against us. Remembering that God is our model (we forgive as God forgave us), we want to follow His lead.

My wife and son and I were sitting at the dinner table catching up on our days. Linda had made a delicious meal of pulled pork. As we ate and talked, Nathan got a piece of the pulled pork on his cheek. He was relating something in conversation that was pretty serious. Linda and I were intent on giving him the attention that the issue deserved. I looked over at my wife, and I saw her trying her best not to break the seriousness of the moment by laughing. Finally, we couldn't hold it in any longer. We had to tell Nathan about the rogue piece of pork so we could pay attention to what he was saying.

That's the way it works when people sin against us. We cannot look at them without seeing their sin. In forgiving us we are told that God removes our sin from us as far as the east is from the west (Ps. 103:12). How far is that, east from west? They are polar opposites. The person and the sin are put at opposite ends. To look at one is not to look at the other. When we forgive we disassociate the sin from the person. The piece of pulled pork is not only taken off, it is taken out of sight.

In Isaiah 38:17 we are told that God "casts" all our sins behind His back. Of course, God is spirit and has no back or body. But He speaks in these anthropomorphic terms to accommodate Himself to our understanding. How well can you see something behind your back? You can't, and that is precisely the point. It is out of sight, no longer associated with the person—by virtue of the act of forgiveness.

How do we maintain that position? So often, we remove an offense but want to keep it in a drawer to retrieve when we want advantage. In fact, we may well have a drawer full of such transgressions, neatly organized by offense like so many pairs of socks. But genuine forgiveness owns no such drawer. The sin is jettisoned. That leads us to the other action involved in forgiving.

TWO STEPS OF FORGIVENESS

As God for Christ's sake hath forgiven you.
—Ephesians 4:32

Remove the offense (Ps. 103:12; Isa. 38:17)
Remember it no more (Isa. 43:25)

>   Offender (1 Cor. 13:5)
>   Others (Prov. 17:9)
>   Ourselves (Phil. 4:8)

The first step to granting forgiveness is to no longer hold the offense against the person who sinned against us. The other shoe to forgiveness, the second action in this walk of love, is to remember the sin no more. In the first place, we separate the offense from the person, removing it from him. In the second we purpose to not remember it any longer. Remove and not remember comprise the two steps of forgiving someone.

Notice we did not say to *forget* the sin. "Forgive and forget" is not a biblical concept. It sounds good and appropriate on the surface, but it presents us with an untenable demand. The language of Scripture is better expressed not as forgive and forget, but as forgive and not remember. We can't flick a switch and forget, but we can work at not remembering.

As we've seen, God is our exemplar in the practice of forgiveness. Notice how His forgiveness is expressed: "I, even I, am he that blotteth out thy transgressions for mine own sake, and will not remember thy sins" (Isa. 43:25; cf. Jer. 31:34). How do we go about not remembering? Not remembering works on the principle that whatever we don't feed will die. Have you ever had an itch, perhaps caused by something like poison ivy? What happens when you scratch it? It becomes inflamed. It calls for more urgent attention, which leads to more inflammation. But if you don't scratch it, what happens? It dies down and heals. It no longer clamors for your attention.

We work at not remembering by not scratching. We feed it no more by no longer bringing it up. This cuts three ways.[4]

One, we no longer bring it up to the *person* we forgave. After all, didn't we forgive him? Isn't the

---

4. I am indebted to Jay E. Adams for this emphasis.

guilt of his offense no longer available to us? Didn't we cast it in the rubbish bin rather than store it in a drawer? This sort of forgiveness is an exercise of love. Love keeps no record of wrongs (1 Cor. 13:5). Accosting a person with an offense that we have "forgiven" him now makes *us* the ones sinning against him.

Two, we no longer bring it up to *others*. That's called gossip, and it is insidiously destructive. It burns as a wildfire, enflaming our hearts, engulfing other relationships. The writer of Proverbs cautions us: "He that covereth a transgression seeketh love; but he that repeateth a matter separateth very friends" (Prov. 17:9).

Three, we no longer bring it up to *ourselves*. Like that itch that begs for our attention, we refuse to scratch. We do not allow it audience in our minds, though it clamor for attention. We follow the counsel of Paul, who instructs us what should occupy our thoughts: "Finally, brethren, whatsoever things are true, whatsoever things are honest, whatsoever things are just, whatsoever things are pure, whatsoever things are lovely, whatsoever things are of good report; if there be any virtue, and if there be any praise, think on these things" (Phil. 4:8). Rather than thinking destructive thoughts, we want to fill our minds with constructive thoughts. The thrust is not so much positive thinking as it is profitable thinking, thinking that edifies and contributes to the goal of peace. We want to take every thought captive to the obedience of Christ (2 Cor. 10:5).

Through these three aspects—not bringing the offense up to the person, to others, or to ourselves— we work at not remembering. By God's grace over time the force of the offense will weaken and perhaps even die. We want to drop it in the grave, cover it with love, and leave it buried with no grave marker to remind us of it. Perhaps it will be forgotten, but at the very least it will be recognized as dead.

What about those times when the person who sinned against us doesn't ask for forgiveness? Ideally, when one has sinned against another the two will meet in the middle, on their way to seek reconciliation. Our Lord starts each out on the path in Matthew 5:24 and 18:15 with the command to "go." However, there are those times we will not make mountains out of molehills or act to address a wrong for what we perceive a greater good. In those times we exercise the discretion of *unilateral* forgiveness.

Proverbs gives us instruction in such forgiveness. "Hatred stirreth up strifes, but love covereth all sins" (Prov. 10:12). "To cover" (*kasah*) is to destroy or overpower, to hide and keep hidden. The psalmist extols the blessing of hidden sin, no longer available for accusation: "Blessed is he whose transgression is forgiven, whose sin is covered. Blessed is the man unto whom the LORD imputeth not iniquity" (Ps. 32:1–2). We cover the sin of those who sin against us by the application of forgiveness in the exercise of love.

We unilaterally purpose not to hold it against the offender any longer and to work at not remembering.

Forgiveness is decidedly Christian, reflecting the One most grievously sinned against. Only by the grace of God bound up in Jesus Christ can we approximate such forgiveness. We shake our heads with astonishment to hear Jesus' answer to Peter, "seventy times seven." We can hear ourselves protesting. "You mean, when they do the same thing?" "Shouldn't I wait to see if they change, if they really meant it?" "Wouldn't it be wise to make them squirm a bit? After all, they need to know how much they hurt me—or at least how wrong they were."

This begs the question of how unilateral forgiveness can work if our Lord makes repentance by the offending party a requisite for our granting forgiveness. Jesus says to His disciples in Luke 17:3–4: "Take heed to yourselves: If thy brother trespass against thee, rebuke him; and if he repent, forgive him. And if he trespass against thee seven times in a day, and seven times in a day turn again to thee, saying, I repent; thou shalt forgive him" (Luke 17:3–4). Is it necessary that we wait on an expression of repentance in order to grant forgiveness? Our Lord does say, "*If he repent*, forgive him."

Jesus' teaching stresses that forgiveness is a reflex of grace received. Having been forgiven is to predispose us to be forgiving of others. What our Lord emphasizes in His instruction to the disciples in Luke 17 is not conditional forgiveness but liberal grace. He is not establishing repentance as a requirement to the granting of forgiveness. Rather, He is breaking down the disciples' narrow, stilted understanding of it and, in so doing, enlarging their understanding of the lavish grace of God.

Jesus is answering the question of how often we are required to forgive, not upon what condition we are required to forgive. We are not told to forgive *if* a brother repents, but *when* a brother repents. In Matthew 18:21, Peter makes no mention of repentance, just how many times he must forgive his offending brother.

Moreover, repentance involves more than simply saying the words "I repent," or "I'm sorry." Three words associated with repentance found in the New Testament flesh out its meaning to include godly sorrow, a reorientation of mind, and a change of direction. Godly sorrow has to do with grief over the harm to another, as opposed to a worldly sorrow that is concerned only for consequences to self. True repentance will result in the fruit, the outworking of a reversal of mind in changed behavior. But, as we've seen, serial forgiveness ("seven times a day") does not allow time to examine the fruit of repentance in order to test its genuineness (see 2 Cor. 7:10–11).

In speaking of seven times a day (Luke 17:4) or seventy times seven (Matt. 18:22), Jesus is not so much laying out the parameters or mechanics for the expression of forgiveness as He is displaying the lavish nature of grace, in the model of God. He is

showcasing an extravagant grace. This is borne out
by the disciples' response to the bar Jesus raises:
"And the apostles said unto the Lord, Increase our
faith" (Luke 17:5). They recognized their insuf-
ficiency for the task and cast themselves on the
sufficiency of Christ.

So our Lord's instruction does not preclude
unilateral forgiveness. We are able to forgive unilaterally, without a response of repentance from the one
who offended us. We can apply the principle of love
in keeping no record of wrongs through the application of the grace of forgiveness. We can disassociate
the offense from the person who has wronged us
and work at not remembering it by not bringing it
up to him, to others, or to ourselves. In so doing, we
dispense grace and we free ourselves from harboring
any bitterness that grows to choke out our own love
and joy and peace.

However, that does not mean there is no place
for repentance. Unilateral forgiveness is real forgiveness, but it is lacking. It is *actual* forgiveness, but it
is not *transactional* forgiveness. Either for reasons of
triviality (e.g., a minor matter) or opportunity (e.g.,
unwillingness of the other), interaction with the
offending party does not take place. Our granting
of forgiveness on our own accord addresses wrongs
from our end, but it does not work to pursue any
reconciliation needed.

Repentance has a place in transactional forgiveness, warranted because repentance recognizes a

wrong. It brings to the table the idea of "sinned against." Repentance flavors David's confession in Psalm 51: "Against thee, thee only, have I sinned, and done this evil in thy sight, that thou mightest be justified when thou speakest, and be clear when thou judgest" (v. 4). Repentance recognizes a fault, a sin against us by another (Matt. 18:15). It takes ownership of its actions and recognizes the reality of an offense.

In a breach of relationship, our goal and desire should be transactional forgiveness. But when that is not possible, for whatever reason, we can employ unilateral forgiveness. In so doing, we allow no root of bitterness to spring up in our own hearts, and we dispose ourselves to grant forgiveness, praying that our God would bring the healing that only He can accomplish.

We want to consider one last aspect, recalling that forgiveness deals with a rupture of that which was whole. Forgiveness is not an end point; rather it is a pivot point. It paves the way for something new.

NOT A CONCLUSION BUT A COMMENCEMENT
The Work of Forgiveness

When we grant forgiveness, we have not finished. We have just entered a new phase. Like removing a splinter and cleaning out the wound, forgiveness sets the stage for healing and rebuilding. That rebuilding involves dealing with sin in our own hearts and perhaps in the lives of those we have forgiven. It entails reestablishing some degree of relationship that, as far as it depends on us, honors Jesus Christ (see Rom. 12:18).

Asking for forgiveness is different from apologizing. Apologizing admits faults and perhaps even expresses regret. Seeking forgiveness does these but also requires an exchange with the one sinned against. When we say, "I apologize," it requires no response. But to say, "Will you forgive me?" puts the ball in the other person's court and involves him or her in the reconciliation process. Apologizing acts to dismiss a grievance. Pursuing forgiveness sets us on a course of peace.

In a sense, to grant forgiveness is to conduct a business transaction centered on the debt of someone's sin against us. For that reason, we may not feel like forgiving the offender, but we purpose to do it. Just as Scripture can command love, so it can command granting forgiveness. It is something we can act on in obedience. Some will say to forgive without feeling like it is hypocritical. However, just like we might not feel like getting out of bed in the morning to go to work but do so anyway because we know we should, we can forgive as a responsible expression of love to God and neighbor.

Forgiveness takes work. It cannot be flippant or perfunctory. It reaches to more than forcing our children to begrudgingly say "sorry" when they commit an offense against a playmate. It must be from the heart, as our Lord emphasizes in Matthew 18:35, and that takes work and begins with a heart inclined toward God. The heart is where we plant the seed that by God's grace will grow into a thing of beauty. Forgiveness uproots destructive weeds such as bitterness and resentment.

When Ellen refused to forgive her abusive father, at issue was more than getting her to say through clenched teeth, "I forgive him." Especially with such a deep and profound hurt, forgiving would set her on a hard road that needed repair. It would be slow going like traveling through a construction zone on the highway, exercising caution and circumspection but slowly moving ahead. But it is a journey that must be undertaken, with her Lord by her side, His grace as her fuel, and His glory as her goal.

The writer of Hebrews charts our course as he directs us to Christ:

> Wherefore seeing we also are compassed about with so great a cloud of witnesses, let us lay aside every weight, and the sin which doth so easily beset us, and let us run with patience the race that is set before us, looking unto Jesus the author and finisher of our faith; who for the joy that was set before him endured the cross, despising the shame, and is set down at the right hand of the throne of God. (Heb. 12:1–2)

Christ is our example. We are to forgive as we have been forgiven. Forgiveness is neither easy nor cheap. It comes at great cost and requires great purpose. *Christ is our strength.* We are to find our ability in Him. Only by abiding in Him can we root out spiritual cancer, find healing, and be instruments of healing. *Christ is our Lord.* We are to follow His desire for our lives and not our own. Our feelings and preferences are real, but they cannot rule the day. These are the sorts of things we remind ourselves of as we cultivate a forgiving spirit in our hearts in running the race set before us, a race that involves relationships.

Forgiveness, the Outworking of Love
To the Colossians, Paul describes love as the overgarment of forgiveness (Col. 3:14). Forgiveness covers over, but it is not a cover up. It is not dismissive of sin. It neither excuses sin nor is an enabler to sin. It is correct to say that we forgive someone's sin, but it is more precise to say that we absolve the guilt of the sin. We forgive the debt incurred by the sin. We remove its offense.

There may well remain consequences, ramifications, and repercussions that we must deal with. A criminal may find forgiveness from the one against whom he committed a crime, but may still face a penalty and still have to make restitution.

Granting forgiveness does not mean that efforts at resolution or reconciliation are lost to us because we removed the offense and must work at not remembering it. To accomplish the rebuilding, restorative goals of forgiveness, we may need to bring the offense to the table. The difference is that the offense is now brought forward for healing rather than for harm. Figuratively speaking, instead of the parties being separated by the offense on the table, they are on the same side of the table working together to deal with it. They are allied against a mutual foe, that the evil one might not find a foothold (see Eph. 4:27).

When someone sins against us multiple times and we forgive him seventy times seven, though we have set aside the guilt, we may have to deal with the issue of heart and practice in that person's life. Granting forgiveness does not guarantee instant trust. Keeping no record of wrongs does not induce a naivety or ignore tendencies. If someone has stolen from us, we are likely to keep our eyes peeled. Jesus was not ignorant about what was in people's hearts and neither should we be.

If Ellen were to take the momentous step toward forgiving her abusive father, that would not be the end of the story. Not only would she embark on much soul-searching through the help of the divine Comforter, she would also be compelled to pursue the sin of her father, at the very least by praying for him, if not confronting him.

When we forgive, we are to put on love. Jesus commands us to love even our enemies. That doesn't mean we are called to generate a rosy, warm feeling toward them or become best buddies. But it does mean we seek our God for a godly attitude and a relationship that honors Him. The Scriptures put loving our enemies in tangible terms driven by God's agenda, as these examples illustrate.

> Thou shalt not avenge, nor bear any grudge against the children of thy people, but thou shalt love thy neighbor as thyself: I am the LORD. (Lev. 19:18)

> But I say unto you which hear, Love your enemies, do good to them which hate you, bless them that curse you, and pray for them which despitefully use you. And unto him that smiteth thee on the one cheek offer also the other; and him that taketh away thy cloke forbid not to take thy coat also. Give to every man that asketh of thee; and of him that taketh away thy goods ask them not again. And as ye would that men should do to you, do ye also to them likewise. For if ye love them which love you, what thank have ye? for sinners also love those that love them. And if ye do good to them which do good to you, what thank have ye? for sinners also do even the same. (Luke 6:27–33)

> Bless them which persecute you: bless, and curse not. Rejoice with them that do rejoice, and weep with them that weep. Be of the same mind one toward another. Mind not high things, but condescend to men of low estate. Be not wise in your own conceits. Recompense to no man evil for evil. Provide things honest in the sight of all men. If it be possible, as much as lieth in you, live peaceably with all men. Dearly beloved, avenge not yourselves, but rather give place unto wrath: for it is written, Vengeance is mine; I will repay, saith the Lord. Therefore if thine enemy hunger, feed

him; if he thirst, give him drink: for in so doing thou shalt heap coals of fire on his head. Be not overcome of evil, but overcome evil with good. (Rom. 12:14–21)

Love is expressed in *practical* terms designed to treat fellow sinners as image bearers of God rather than as objects of our hate. Scripture holds out for us a minimum comportment for our treatment of others, even though we may never recover any level of intimacy with them.

Forgive and Never Forget

Following the conquest of the Promised Land under the leadership of Joshua, the Reubenites, Gadites, and the half tribe of Manasseh set out to return to their land on the east of the Jordan River. Before they crossed the Jordan, however, they paused to build an altar of imposing size.

Hearing that, the nine-and-a-half tribes that remained in the land of Canaan mobilized for war. They gathered themselves before the two-and-a-half tribes and accused them of treason against the Lord their God. The trans-Jordanian tribes responded with great vehemence that they were doing no such thing. Rather, they had erected the altar, not for sacrifice, but as a remembrance that they, too, were part of the people of Israel. Once the memories of war had faded they did not want the descendants on either side to think that the natural boundary of the Jordan River suggested a division among the people of God.

They laid out their reasoning:

> Therefore said we, that it shall be, when they should so say to us or to our generations in time to come, that we may say again, Behold the pattern of the altar of the LORD, which our fathers made, not for burnt offerings, nor for sacrifices; but it is a witness between us and you. God forbid that we should rebel against the LORD, and turn this day from following the LORD, to build an altar for burnt offerings, for meat offerings, or for sacrifices, beside the altar of the LORD our God that is before his tabernacle. (Josh. 22:28–29)

In like fashion, our Lord has given us an altar, not of sacrifice, but of remembrance. It harkens to the true altar on which sacrifice was made, the cross of Calvary that held the Lamb of God who takes away the sin of the world. Those who partake of the elements remember His death until He returns, not as a sacrifice for sin once again, but to claim those for whom He died.

This altar of remembrance is the Communion table, around which is celebrated the Lord's Supper. Those assembled commune together with a living Lord. They point to His atoning death for the remission of their sin and proclaim unity among those of kindred faith. "The cup of blessing which we bless, is it not the communion of the blood of Christ? The bread which we break, is it not the communion of the body of Christ? For we being many are one bread, and one body: for we are all partakers of that one bread" (1 Cor. 10:16–17).

This "altar" stands as a constant reminder of where our forgiveness is found and of the need to forgive as we have been forgiven, in reminder that we are one body. Every time we celebrate the sacrament, we hear the voice of our Lord: "Is there an offense you are holding onto against a brother or sister in Christ? Are you refusing to forgive the puddle of sin against you, even though I forgave the ocean of your sin against Me? Let it go. If you can't, then go, with haste. Leave the offerings you brought. Be reconciled to your brother. Then come and worship Me, the God of peace."